D0405293

Whisker Wisdom

The Teachings of
Two Small Siamese ~~Boys~~ *Girls*

R. W. Brooks

Whisker Wisdom ™

Orders: www.whiskerwisdom.com

Copyright © 2008 by R.W. Brooks
ISBN- 1-57438-071-0

Printed in Prescott, Arizona
EMI PrintWorks

Preface

Most books about teaching animals involve techniques on how people train or modify an animal's behavior.

This book reverses those priorities. It is about how two small Siamese kittens taught me about being in the moment, about being aware of my many blessings, and most of all, about love.

The pictures were taken by the author using a simple digital camera. They were not staged — but were taken at opportune moments capturing "kitties being kitties".

iii

A cat isn't fussy–just so long as
you remember she likes her milk
in the shallow, rose-patterned
saucer and her fish on the blue
plate. From which she will take
it, and eat it off the floor

Arthur Bridges

iv

In Memory

"Sissy"

Sissy was a wonderful companion for 22 years. She was indeed a blessing in my life and her many gifts will be remembered and cherished.

It's only when we truly know
and understand that we have a
limited time on earth~~~and that
we have no way of knowing
when our time is up~~~that we
will begin to live each day to the
fullest, as if it was the only one
we had

Elisabeth Kubler-Ross

Contents

Preface   iii

In Memory   v

Contents   vii

Explanation   9

Introduction   15

Meet the Girls   19

The Teachings   31

   Be in the Present   33

   Learning to Play   49

   Don't Take Life Too Seriously   65

Being Grateful	81
How to be a Loving Dad	95
Just Being Kitties	113
In Closing	123
In Gratitude	125
Ordering Information	127

Explanation

OK! OK! ....before we get to the "Wisdom Stuff", the "boys....girls" thing needs to be clarified.

I first found out about the "boys" from an online listing which stated that there were nine BOY Siamese kittens for sale from a local breeder.

I had decided that two kittens would be preferable to one, so that I would not have the responsibility of parenting a one child family. I am an only child and know how much a brother or sister would have meant to me in terms of having someone to talk and play with. The sex of the kitties was not a factor in making a choice.

I met all nine "brothers" at the breeder's home. They were actually two litters with a common father, and about 8 to 9 weeks old. They were cute!!! Little fluff balls with blue eyes; all but two were in a blanketed box with one of the mothers. The other two were out adventuring in the kitchen playing a game of chase. Well, those are the two I chose to bring home.

I contacted the "Visiting Vet", Dr. Ann Ferens, who came to my home, examined the kitties and administered their first shots. She advised me that the kittens were healthy and that there were no observable testicles at this time; she also said that it often takes a few weeks for these characteristics to manifest.

Dr. Ann came to my home in about 6 weeks to administer the second round of kitty shots. Upon her arrival, the kittens promptly ran under the bed.....Smart Kitties! They had already determined that the "scent" of Dr. Ann was associated with the not so pleasant experience of having objects inserted, including temperature taking devices. I was able to coax ("grab") the "boys" from under the bed and they received their injections without a whimper. Dr. Ann was still not able to determine the kitties' sex. She offered to return in about a month and check the "boys" again, since the time for neutering surgery was not too far away.

Dr. Ann examined the kitties when they were about five months old and emphatically stated, "These are Girls!!!!" What a Surprise!!!!

The Blessing

When I was at the Breeder's home, she stated that *if* the kittens I selected were *"Female", she would have kept them* for breeding purposes.

The Universe works in mysterious and wonderful ways. We may not always understand happenings at the moment, but things always happen for the "highest good" of all concerned.

Well, that explains the "sex change" in the Title and how very fortunate I was to have two wonderful "Girls" to love. The girls are also fortunate in that they are in a home where they are cherished and don't have to compete for food or space. What a win-win situation.

Cats are Wonderful Friends

Gentle eyes that see so much,
Paws that have the quiet touch,
Purrs to signal "all is well"
And show more love than words could tell.
Graceful movements touched with pride,
A calming presence by our side.
A friendship that takes time to grow
Small wonder why we love them so.

Author Unknown

14

Introduction

I knew when I brought these two little Angels with four feet to their new home, that the Universe had bestowed a very special and wonderful blessing—A gift which would continue to be one of amazement, inspiration, healing, and joy in my life.

They came to me at a time when my life was at a very low ebb—my health was failing, I had no real purpose in living and my creative ventures were pretty much limited to watching TV and going to the market. The strangling grip of depression was devastating. I was no longer doing volunteer work, creating beautiful wooden vessels on the lathe, or, for that matter, involved with people.

Just leaving home to do simple errands was accompanied with a great deal of trepidation and reluctance.

Much of that condition has changed since the girls have been here. First of all, I had two little kittens whom depended on me for food, water, shelter, love, and a kitty box (make that a *clean* kitty box).

Secondly, I became fascinated with their abilities to adapt to new and strange surroundings, be comfortable with being separated from seven other brothers and their mother, and learning where to eat and poop in such a brief period of time. Finally, they did all of this with a sense of adventure and bonding which continues to grow to this day.

I did not realize at the time that these two special girls would also be a source of wisdom, courage, healing, and growth; and that their "teachings" would have a profound effect on my perceptions, values, and quality of life.

Whisker Wisdom is a story of how two tiny Siamese kittens taught me to laugh again, be grateful for many blessings, and not take life too seriously. It is also a story about how these two four-pawed angels rekindled my ability to both give and receive love.

The writing of this book is my "***Victory Statement***"of overcoming the severe depression which consumed so much of my life and how the kitties were such a part of this wonderful transition.

I hope in some way the "teachings" offered on the following pages will touch your heart, facilitate healing as needed, and bring more joy into your life.

R.W. Brooks

Meet the Girls

Most human babies are given names prior to birth. This was not the case with the girls. I wanted their names to reflect some characteristic or mannerism unique to each kitten. It took about 3 weeks before the names "Hunter" and "Pur" evolved.

Hunter has a very sleek body and is the lighter of the two kitties. She has almond shaped eyes and has unique color rings on her tail ("Ringo" was a name under consideration). She is very cautious and tends to stalk her toys, including her own tail. Her hunting posture led to her name.

Pur is more traditional in her Siamese characteristics. She has a somewhat rounded face, and of course, big blue round eyes. If she were a person, she would be a poster child in some advertisement for baby food! She has a very loud purr and exhibits her happiness quite often, especially when held and being petted; thus, Pur was a perfect name.

Hunter has many interests including: watching anything that moves, climbing, chasing Pur and her own tail, and tearing up toilet paper. Her favorite toys include a somewhat battered cloth mouse, a leather shoe lace and pieces of ribbon. Her most embarrassing moment was when she fell off of the T.V.

Pur also has a variety of interests including: smelling and eating rose petals, hiding in boxes, chasing Hunter and her own tail, and playing tag. Her favorite toys are a toothbrush, a ping pong ball and her own tacky-looking brown mouse. Her most embarrassing moment was when she was walking on top of the shower (a ledge less than 1" wide) and fell off into the toilet!

The past cannot be regained,
although we can learn from it;
the future is not yet ours even
though we must plan for
it…Time is now. We have only
today.

Charles Hummel

Hunter wants to be a writer

If my heart can become pure
and simple like that of a child, I
think there probably can be no
greater happiness in life

Kitaro Nishida

Pur wants to be a Dentist

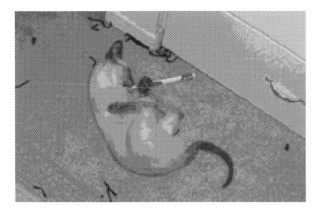

A dream is in the mind of the believer, and in the hands of the doer. You are not given a dream, without being given the power to make it come true

Anonymous

Hunter has been here!

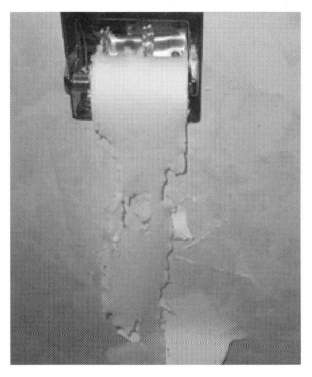

Life begins as a quest of the child
for the man and ends as a
journey by the man to
rediscover the child

Laurens Van der Post

28

Pur studies Ornithology....she is always looking at the birds

Patience is the companion of
wisdom

Author Unknown

The Teachings

I have learned or re-focused on many lessons as a result of having Hunter and Pur in my life. These lessons have been grouped under five headings:

Be in the Present
Learning to Play
Don't Take Life Too Seriously
Being Grateful
How to be a Loving Dad

Each lesson will be briefly explained and followed by a series of captioned pictures illustrating the lesson in a light-hearted manner.

An opportunity for you, the reader, to actively participate in the lesson will follow each picture section. I hope that the "Try This" activities will be both entertaining and meaningful for you! (I was a teacher for 22 years and could not resist the temptation to include some type of teaching-learning activity in this book).

With this brief description completed, let's move on to "The Lessons".

Be in the
Present

This day is all that is good and fair. It is too dear, with its hopes and invitations, to waste a moment on the yesterdays

Ralph Waldo Emerson

Be in the Present

Kitties and all other animals, except humans, live totally in the present moment. They don't worry about what might happen or fret over past events. They are not caught up in the "shoulda, "woulda", "coulda" syndrome. Instead, they are totally focused on what is happening right now.

It has never ***not been*** the present moment! We have the ability to be aware of which time frame we are in; in doing so, we ***are in*** the present moment.

John Lennon once said, " *Life* is what's happening while we're busy making other plans". Now is the only time we have and the only time we have control over. Fear is always about what might happen and regret is always past oriented. Mark Twain was quoted as saying, "I have been through some terrible things in my life......some of which actually happened".

There is no better time to be happy than the present; so, practice being a kitty!

Kitties don't multi-task

To do two things at once is to do neither

Publilius Syrus

Be focused 100% on what you are doing

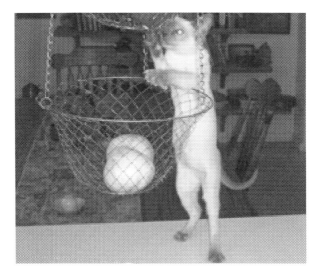

You've got to do your own
growing, no matter how tall
your grandfather was

Irish Proverb

Pur enjoys the SuperBowl

You miss 100% of the shots you
don't take

Wayne Gretsky

The only time is now

If we are ever to enjoy life, now
is the time, not tomorrow or
next year…
Today should always be our
most wonderful day

Thomas Dreier

Who doesn't like to snuggle in a pile of clean, warm clothes

Way down deep, we're all motivated by the same urges. Cats have the courage to live by them

Jim Davis

Try This

When you wake up tomorrow, ask
yourself the following question:

*In order for what I do today to be
remembered as a "very special day of
my life", what do I need to do to make
it so? What am I going to do today to
make it special? Act on these
thoughts during the day.*

*Before retiring for the evening,
review the events of your day and
ask yourself, "What makes some of
these "special"?*
*You may wish to repeat this exercise
the following day(s).*

We can easily forgive a child
who is afraid of the dark; the
real tragedy of life is when men
are afraid of the light

Plato

Learning to Play

Cats are intended to teach us
that not everything in nature has
a function

Author Unknown

Learning to Play

Kittens have a marvelous way of learning life and survival skills—They Play! Whether it's 'chasing tails', pouncing upon an imitation mouse, playing 'hide and seek', or slowly creeping up on the 'shoelace snake', the learning takes place having fun.

Play serves people in many of the same ways as it does animals. People have also used some form of play to make work easier or to better tolerate unpleasant conditions.

As a teacher of children often living in extreme poverty, I was (and am)

amazed at how they could play and laugh despite their poor living conditions.

By watching Hunter and Pur engage in hours of play, I have become more at ease, see humor in many more situations, and have fun doing many tasks that I once considered boring and difficult.

Thanks to my 'girls', I am quickly learning how to play—as an adult; it is never too late to learn. The rewards are improved health, both physical and mental.

You're never too old to play

53

Each day, and the living of it,
has to be a conscious creation in
which discipline and order are
relieved with some play and
pure foolishness

Mary Sarton

Golf is great fun

The Gods too are fond of a joke

Aristotle

It's Wonderful Having a Play Partner

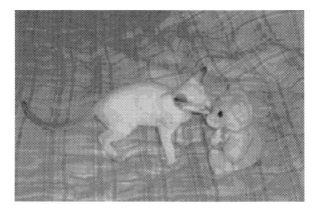

The most effective kind of education is that a child should play amongst lovely things

Plato

Kitties love to play "hide and seek"

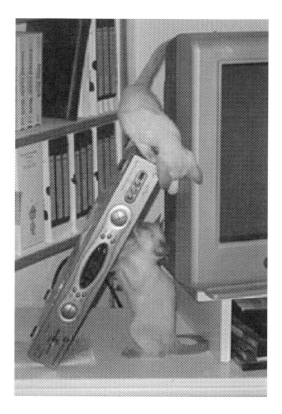

Humor is the great thing, the
saving thing. The minute it
crops up, all our irritations and
resentments slip away and a
sunny spirit takes their place

Mark Twain

We like to play "jungle" kitties

61

If you are not playful you are
not alive

David Hockney

Try This

There is an old saying which says, "If you want to learn how to do something—Teach It!"

Given the understanding that the ability to play is inherent in all of us, how would you facilitate a group of adults who are reluctant to let themselves play? What specific things would you ask them to do? (especially in the beginning lessons)

You can keep a dog; but it is the cat who keeps people, because cats find humans useful domestic animals

George Mikes

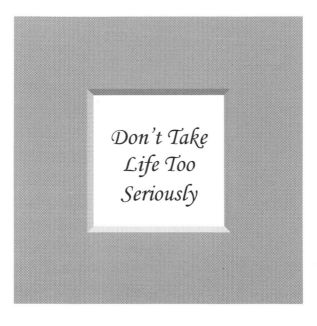

*Don't Take
Life Too
Seriously*

When you encounter difficulties
and contradictions, do not try to
break them, but bend them with
gentleness and time

Saint Francis de Sales

Do Not Take Life Too Seriously

In many cases there is an inverse relationship between how seriously a person approaches life and their ability to play and have fun. There is a significant difference between being rigid and being focused. A person can be loose and still keep on task.

I was the type of person who approached every event, even play, as if it were a life or death scenario. In doing so, the joy of the moment was lost. Fear—fear of success and/or fear of failure is at the core of this problem. As a result, most of my present time was occupied with past or future happenings.

Life is designed to be adventurous and fun—It is a game in which no one comes out alive! Do you want to arrive at death 'safely', as if all living was a gauntlet, or leave this World with a smile on your face, a few cuts and bruises, and your bank account just arriving at $0.00?

When good things happen often and with ease, we tend to think something must be wrong because we did not suffer or work hard enough to have such an outcome. Outdated thinking states that anything worth having must take a long time to achieve and there must be a certain amount of pain associated with this accomplishment---No Pain...No Gain!

Stress can be defined as the difference between what we *have* and what we *want.* The greater the difference—the greater the amount of stress and vice-versa. There will be times when our expectations will not be met and, unfortunately, many people lead unhappy lives because things, people, or events are not in line with their expectations. Letting go of unrealistic expectations and 'rolling with the punches' will bring more inner peace and freedom.

Life is not an emergency (most of the time). I believed for many years that my happiness was dependent on completing each and every task perfectly—as if my life depended upon it; little things were given emergency status. I took achieving goals so seriously that fun was eliminated.

The learning of life lessons in a playful and yet focused way by Pur and Hunter caused me to step back and view life as *a practice session*. Now, challenges have become opportunities to grow and not a serious battle to be won. Thank you Girls!

Hey! Get over on your side of the bed!

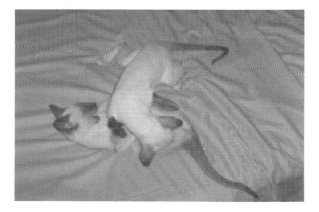

Cats seem to go on the principle
that it never does any harm to
ask for what you want

Joseph Wood Krutch

Did you hear the one about......

He deserves Paradise who makes
his companions laugh

Koran

Now, this is how you do it.....Watch Me!

There are two means of refuge
from the miseries of life: music
and cats

Albert Schweitzer

Oh My! You have "killer breath"

The chief danger in life is that
you may take too many
precautions

Alfred Adler

Try This

In a dream you are near death and are regretting all the things you did not do in your lifetime, mainly because you were always 'too busy'.

A little voice instructs you to write down these regrets. Then you are given some great news: "You have been given a 5—year life extension pass."

What are you going to do with this new opportunity?

It's never too late to be what you might have been

George Eliot

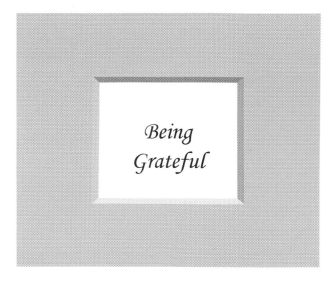

Being
Grateful

Reflect upon your present blessings—of which every man has many—not on your past misfortunes, of which all men have some

Charles Dickens

Being Grateful

We have become a society which takes many things for granted and believes that life comes with certain guarantees and entitlements. It is very difficult to be grateful with this type of belief system. Unfortunately, the 'what have you done for me lately' attitude is quite prevalent in modern times.

The true expression of gratefulness is Joy! Being grateful is a function of the heart and not the brain. Unfortunately, we are not grateful for something we value unless we lose or don't have it. Good health and the

83

lack of it is an appropriate example and one which I have personally experienced.

We also tend to focus on what we lack or don't have instead of expressing thanks for all the blessing we do have.

The more we become aware of all that we actually have and express sincere gratitude, the more good will come into our lives. In essence, the more we sincerely give from the heart, the more we receive from a bountiful Universe.

Be thankful that you can love!

Count your blessings, not your crosses,
Count your gains, not your losses.
Count your joys instead of your woes,
Count your friends instead of your foes.
Count your health, not your wealth.

Old Proverb

86

It's great having a Sister!

If we learn how to give of ourselves, to forgive others, and to live with thanksgiving, we need not seek happiness. It will seek us.

Anonymous

It's great to have someone cover your "backside"

Gratitude is not only the
greatest of virtues, but the
parent of all others

Cicero

You scratch my back and I'll scratch your back!

We make a living by what we get, we make a life by what we give

Sir Winston Churchill

Try This

At the end of each day, write down one thing for which you are extremely grateful. It must be of importance to you. There can be no duplications as you compile your list.

After a week or so, review the items on your list. You should happily notice that there is a greater occurrence or frequency of some of the items listed.

What we are truly grateful for will manifest in greater quantity and quality.

One person reported doing this for several years, and still has not had any duplication!

One small cat changes coming
home to an empty house to
coming home

Pam Brown

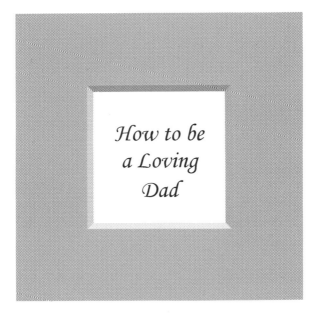

*How to be
a Loving
Dad*

Blessed indeed is the man who
hears many gentle voices call
him father!

Lydia Maria Child

How to be a Loving Dad

I have been given many, many 'parenting' opportunities and lessons raising two small Siamese kittens. These go beyond providing the essentials for life...food, water, shelter, etc. (I am not equating the 'parenting' of my 'girls" to the extremely complex skills required to successfully parent children; however, there are some common elements).

Being 'Dad' to Pur and Hunter has been both a wonderful and challenging experience. After the kitties came to their new home, I began to focus more on their needs and less on my problems. As a consequence, I began to feel better, both physically and mentally, and became more active in living. Watching the girls grow and change increased my reverence for life itself.

We are all created with the ability to love and the need to express that love. I found that it was very easy to love the girls and I cherish their 'essence' as a unique life form and joy in my life. I also believe they are very capable of loving their 'Dad'. If you have ever been close to any pet, you know what that experience feels like. Love is a Universal constant and has no limitations.

Will you love me?

That best portion of a good man's life, His little, nameless, unremembered acts of kindness and love

William Wordsworth

We love our Dad

The supreme happiness in life is
the conviction that we are loved

Victor Hugo

I know where Dad keeps the food......We can raid it tonight!

Any man can be a father, but it takes someone special to be a Dad

Anne Geddes

Trust is an important part of love

The pur from cat to man says,
'you bring me happiness; I am at
peace with you'

Barbara L. Diamond

I think Dad is fix'n dinner for us

You know, fathers just have a
way of putting everything
together

Erika Cosby

Will you tuck me in now?

Purring is an automatic safety
valve device for dealing with
happiness overflow

Anonymous

Try This

Go to a florist and purchase a beautiful bouquet or plant for yourself.

Fill out the gift card with something like:

To: (your name) ...a nice person who_____

_____

You can tell your cat anything
and he'll still love you. If you
lose your job or your best friend,
your cat will think no less of you

Helen Powers

Just Being Kitties

The following captioned pictures depict the kittens doing what they do best: exploring, playing, more playing, learning about their environment and themselves, and providing countless hours of laughter, amazement, and serenity for their "Dad".

Whisker Wisdom

I'm only a cat,
And I stay in my place…
Up there on your chair,
On your bed or your face!

I'm only a cat,
And I don't finick much…
I'm happy with cream
And anchovies and such!

I'm only a cat,
And we'll get along fine…
As long as you know
I'm not yours…you're all mine!

Author Unknown

Pur wants to be a Tiger

None of us will ever accomplish anything excellent or commanding except when he listens to this whisper which is heard by him alone

Ralph Waldo Emerson

What is that "smell"? Did that come from you?

The goal of life is living in
agreement with Nature

Zeno

118

I am my Daddy's Girl!

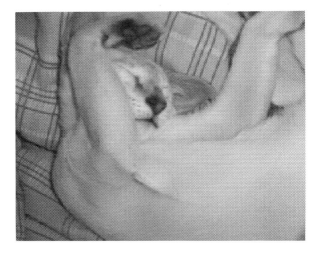

Thousands of years ago, cats
were worshipped as gods. Cats
have never forgotten this

Anonymous

Did *you* do that?

A cat has absolute emotional honesty; human beings, for one reason or another, may hide their feelings, but a cat does not

Ernest Hemingway

In Closing

Thank you for reading about Hunter and Pur and their teachings.

I hope you found their story to be both entertaining and enlightening.

May your pets bring you many wonderful and unforgettable experiences as you love and cherish them.

R.W. Brooks

123

God sleeps in the rock;
Dreams in the plant;
Stirs in the animal;
And awakens in Man

Old Sufi Proverb

In Gratitude

I want to thank my wife, *Gail,* for her support during the writing of this book. She also deserves credit for creating the main title, "Whisker Wisdom".

Lloyd Engdahl, a friend and neighbor, presented many positive suggestions during the writing process. His advice, "just write it down and deal with editing later" inspired me to do just that!

Long-time friend, *Ron Smith*, provided me with much needed information regarding printing and publishing this book.

Finally, blessings to my 'girls', *Pur* and *Hunter*....without them this book would not exist.

When the time is right, the
teacher will appear

Author Unknown

Ordering Information

Additional copies of "Whisker Wisdom" may be ordered at the following website:

www.whiskerwisdom.com